Village School
Language Arts/Social Studies
Department

Texas

by Terri Sievert

Consultant:
Mary G. Ramos
Editor
Texas Almanac

Capstone
press
Mankato, Minnesota

Capstone Press

151 Good Counsel Drive • P.O. Box 669 • Mankato, Minnesota 56002

http://www.capstone-press.com

Printed in the United States of America

Library of Congress Cataloging-in-Publication Data
Sievert, Terri.
    Texas / by Terri Sievert.
    v. cm.—(Land of liberty)
    Includes bibliographical references and index.
    Contents: About Texas—Land, climate, and wildlife—History of Texas—Government and politics—Economy and resources—People and culture.
    ISBN 0-7368-1594-5 (hardcover)
    1. Texas—Juvenile literature. [1. Texas.] I. Title. II. Series.
F386.3 .S54 2003
917.64—dc21   2002010322

Summary: An introduction to the geography, history, government, politics, economy, resources, people, and culture of Texas, including maps, charts, and a recipe.

Editorial Credits

Megan Schoeneberger, editor; Jennifer Schonborn, series designer; Linda Clavel, book designer; Angi Gahler, illustrator; Deirdre Barton, photo researcher; Eric Kudalis, product planning editor

Photo Credits

Cover images: longhorn cattle, Corbis/Wolfgang Kaehler; oil pump, Pixelchrome/Jeremy Woodhouse

American Radio Relay League/Tom A. Griffy, 36; Bruce Coleman Inc./Julie Eggers, 52; Capstone Press, 56; Capstone Press/Gary Sundermeyer, 54; Corbis/Bettmann, 28, 29; Corbis/Dave G. Houser, 46; Corbis/David Muench, 12–13; Corbis/Joe McDonald, 14; Corbis/Joseph Sohm - Visions of America, 50–51; Corbis/Kelly-Mooney Photography, 45; Folio, Inc./Richard Cummins, 18; Getty Images/Hulton Archive, 20, 24, 30–31, 39, 58; Houserstock/Dave G. Houser, 8; Houserstock/J. Butchofsky, 32; Index Stock Imagery/Bob Burch, 4; Index Stock Imagery/Ray Hendley, 40; Library of Congress, 27; One Mile Up, Inc., 55 (both); Panoramic Images/VOA LLC/J. Sohm, 22–23; PhotoDisc, Inc., 1; PhotoDisc, Inc./D. Falconer, 43; Steve Mulligan, 63; Stock Montage, Inc., 16, 38; Unicorn Stock Photos/Jack Milchanowski, 57; U.S. Postal Service, 59

Artistic Effects

Digital Stock, Digital Vision Ltd., PhotoDisc, Inc.

1 2 3 4 5 6 08 07 06 05 04 03

Table of Contents

In a rodeo, riders showcase their skills at handling horses and cattle.

4

Chapter 1

About Texas

One hand raised, the cowboy starts his ride. The horse's rear legs kick into the air, but the cowboy holds on tightly. He tries to ride for eight seconds. Finally, the buzzer sounds, and the crowd cheers.

The cowboy is riding in a rodeo, the state sport of Texas. Rodeo has roots in Texas history. In 1883, cowboys gathered in Pecos, Texas, and tested each other's skills in riding and cattle roping. Texas cowboys and cowgirls turned the friendly games into a sport. Today, a rodeo happens every week somewhere in Texas.

"Texas is a state of mind. Texas is an obsession. Above all, Texas is a nation in every sense of the word."

—John Steinbeck, author

The Lone Star State

Texas is known as the Lone Star State because it has one star on its flag. It is the second largest state in the United States after Alaska. Illinois, Indiana, Iowa, Ohio, and Wisconsin together could fit inside the borders of Texas. The large state ranks second to California in population. More than 20 million people live in Texas.

Texas is in the southwestern United States. Oklahoma is north of Texas. The Texas Panhandle, the part of Texas that reaches northward, is next to the western part of Oklahoma. Arkansas touches the northeastern corner of Texas. The Red River divides Texas from Oklahoma and Arkansas. Louisiana lies to the east of Texas. The Sabine River makes up part of the border between Texas and Louisiana. The Gulf of Mexico washes against the southeastern side of Texas. The Rio Grande divides the state from Mexico in the south and southwest. The Rio Grande border is 1,241 miles (1,997 kilometers) long. New Mexico borders the western side of Texas.

Texas' Cities

Scale
Miles
0   60   120   180   240
0   60   120   180   240   300
Kilometers

NEW MEXICO

OKLAHOMA

ARKANSAS

Red River

Sabine River

• Lubbock

• Dallas

Fort Worth •

LOUISIANA

• El Paso

TIGUA RESERVATION

TEXAS

ALABAMA-COUSHATTA RESERVATION

☆ Austin

Beaumont •

Houston •

San Antonio •

Rio Grande

Galveston •

MEXICO

TEXAS KICKAPOO RESERVATION

Corpus Christi •

Gulf of Mexico

The Rio Grande winds along the border between Texas and Mexico. In some places, the water has cut deep canyons into the rocky land.

Chapter 2

Land, Climate, and Wildlife

Four main land regions cover Texas. They contain rocky land, rich soil, and sandy beaches.

Basin and Range Province

The Basin and Range Province in far western Texas also is called the Trans-Pecos region. There, the land rises into mountains. These mountains are part of the southern tip of the Rocky Mountains. In this area, the highest point in the state, Guadalupe Peak, reaches 8,749 feet (2,667 meters) above sea level.

The Rio Grande is in the southern part of the Basin and Range Province. Rio Grande means "big river" in Spanish. Its fast-flowing waters have cut canyons into the rock. Many of these canyons are in Big Bend National Park.

Great Plains

The Great Plains region covers the Texas Panhandle and central Texas. In the western part of the region, farmers use irrigation to grow cotton and wheat in the Llano Estacado, or Staked Plain.

The Permian Basin is in the southern part of the Great Plains. It has the state's largest supply of petroleum and natural gas.

Rivers run through the Edwards Plateau. This area often is called Hill Country. The rocky hills and canyons there have few bushes or grasses.

Interior Lowlands

The Interior Lowlands region is east of the Great Plains. The area has prairies and lakes. In the past, tall grasses covered the land. Today, farmers use the land for growing crops.

The Eastern and Western Cross Timbers area is part of this region. It divides the Interior Lowlands from the Gulf Coastal

Texas' Land Features

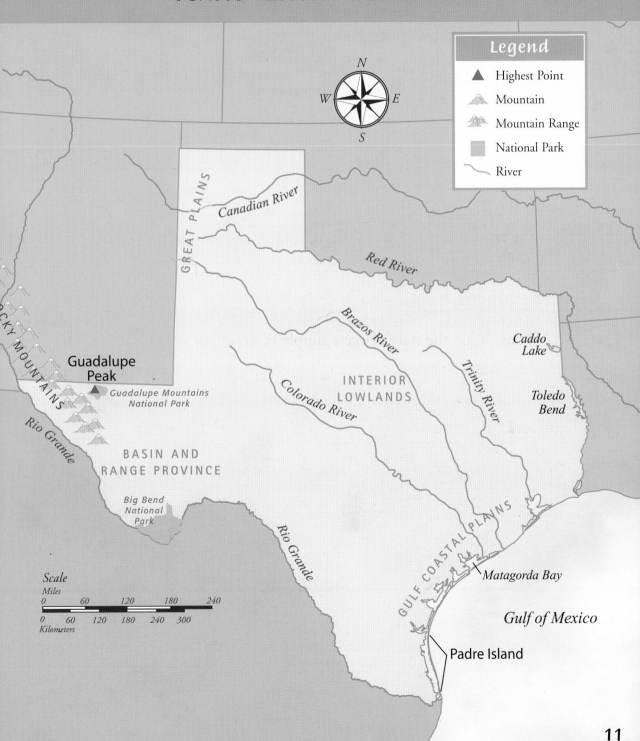

Legend
- ▲ Highest Point
- Mountain
- Mountain Range
- National Park
- River

N
W E
S

GREAT PLAINS

Canadian River

Red River

Brazos River

Caddo Lake

Toledo Bend

ROCKY MOUNTAINS

Guadalupe Peak
▲ Guadalupe Mountains National Park

INTERIOR LOWLANDS

Trinity River

Colorado River

Rio Grande

BASIN AND RANGE PROVINCE

Big Bend National Park

Rio Grande

GULF COASTAL PLAINS

Matagorda Bay

Gulf of Mexico

Padre Island

Scale
Miles
0   60   120   180   240
0   60   120   180   240   300
Kilometers

Plains. Farmers there grow cotton and corn. Oak and hickory forests cover the hills.

The West Texas Rolling Plains region is in the western part of the Interior Lowlands. The area has rich soil. Cattle graze on the hillsides.

Gulf Coastal Plains

The Rio Grande valley continues into the southwestern part of the Gulf Coastal Plains. Mesquite trees and prickly pear cactus cover the plains north of the valley.

The Rio Grande and other rivers flow into the Gulf of Mexico. Long, narrow islands called barrier islands lie along the shore. One barrier island, Padre Island, is 130 miles (209 kilometers) long. At its widest point, it is only 3 miles (4.8 kilometers) wide.

Climate

Texas has varied weather. The Basin and Range Province receives less than 12 inches (30 centimeters) of rain each year. Areas along the Gulf Coast receive up to 50 inches (127 centimeters) of rain

Padre Island is among the barrier islands that lie along the Texas coast. Warm, damp winds from the Gulf of Mexico blow across the coast, keeping the area warm.

13

The Horned Lizard

The horned lizard is the state reptile of Texas. It has pointy spines along its head and back. When attacked, it shoots blood from its eyes to surprise its attacker.

A horned lizard is the subject of a Texan tall tale. According to the story, a horned lizard was placed in the cornerstone of the Eastland County courthouse. City leaders found the sleepy lizard alive 31 years later. Horned lizard experts are sure the story is not true. The lizards live no more than seven years, and like other reptiles, they need sunlight to stay alive.

each year. The coast stays warm all year due to warm, damp winds from the Gulf of Mexico.

Winds blowing across the flat Panhandle bring cold winters and hot summers. In northern Texas, dust storms and sandstorms can block the sun and hurt a person's skin. During winter, up to 24 inches (61 centimeters) of snow can fall in the Panhandle.

Severe weather often strikes the state. Texas has more tornadoes per year than any other state. Hurricanes often

Did you know...?
In 1900, a hurricane in Galveston killed 6,000 people.

sweep in from the Gulf of Mexico during hurricane season from June to November.

Wildlife

Warm winters draw wild birds to Texas. Many birds come to Brazoria National Wildlife Refuge near the Gulf Coast. In mid-December, birders have counted more than 200 types of birds. As many as 50,000 geese and 30,000 ducks also spend winter in the refuge.

Texas is home to many mammals. More than 3 million white-tailed deer graze in wooded areas across Texas. Armadillos, the state small mammal, eat insects and spiders.

Some animals in Texas could die out as people cut down trees and put up buildings in nature areas. Whooping cranes are among the endangered animals. At 5 feet (1.5 meters) tall, they are the tallest birds in Texas. They have a 7.5-foot (2-meter) wingspan. Spotted cats called ocelots once lived in thick, thorny brush in southern Texas and along the coast. Today, only about 35 ocelots live in a protected area near Brownsville. Many slender, solid-colored jaguarundi cats once roamed southern Texas, but few remain.

15

Spanish explorers were the first Europeans to visit Texas. Hernán Cortés, shown here, claimed Texas and Mexico for Spain in 1521.

Chapter 3

History of Texas

American Indians were the first people to live in Texas. The Caddo Indians farmed and lived in villages in eastern Texas. The name Texas comes from the Caddo word for friend. The Apache tribes often fought with settlers and other tribes. They moved often to find food instead of planting crops. The Comanche were excellent horse riders. They hunted buffalo on horseback. Later, the Cherokee, Choctaw, Chickasaw, Creek, Kickapoo, and Shawnee also moved into Texas.

Explorers

Spanish explorers were the first Europeans in Texas. In 1519, Alonso Alvarez de Pineda mapped the Texas coast. He was

Spanish monks built a church in Ysleta to teach Christianity to the American Indians who lived nearby.

looking for a route to the Pacific Ocean. He found the mouth of the Rio Grande. Later, Hernán Cortés claimed Texas and Mexico for Spain. In 1540, Francisco Vasquez de Coronado and more than 1,300 men passed through northern Texas. Some of the men were looking for gold. Other men were missionaries. Spanish monks set up the first Texas settlement in 1682. They founded Ysleta, close to present-day El Paso.

The French also claimed land in Texas. In 1685, René-Robert Cavelier, known as Sieur de La Salle, looked for the mouth of the Mississippi River. Before he could find it, he was shipwrecked in Matagorda Bay. La Salle started a colony on the Gulf Coast. But by 1689, the colony was left empty.

The Spanish continued exploring and settling in the area. They built a fort at the mission of San Antonio de Valero in 1718. In 1772, San Antonio became the center of Spanish government in Texas.

Settlers

In 1820, American Moses Austin asked the Spanish governor for permission to bring settlers into Texas. Austin died before he could bring the settlers, so his son Stephen carried out the plan. He led 300 families to an area between the Brazos River and the Colorado River. They grew cotton and raised sheep. By this time, Spain no longer ruled the area. Mexico, which included Texas, became its own country in 1821.

Many Americans saw a chance for a better life in Texas. The Mexican government worried that American settlers would threaten Mexico's control of Texas. They passed the

Law of April 6, 1830, to make settling in Texas easier for Mexicans but harder for Americans.

Looking for Freedom

Tension grew between U.S. settlers and the Mexican government. The settlers were unhappy with the new law.

Texans fought for their independence from Mexico at the battle of the Alamo.

"I shall never surrender or retreat ... VICTORY OR DEATH."
—William Barret Travis, commander at the Alamo,
in a letter written during the first day of the battle

Stephen Austin went to Mexico City to ask ruler General Antonio López de Santa Anna to allow more Americans into Texas. Before Austin could return home, Mexican officials found a letter from Austin to American settlers. The letter was about Texas becoming its own country. Austin was arrested and jailed from 1833 to 1835.

The Texas Revolution began in 1835. Mexican troops tried to take a cannon from Gonzales, Texas. The settlers refused to give them the cannon, and fighting began.

Remember the Alamo

More than four months later, the revolution's most famous battle began. On February 23, 1836, some Texans had taken shelter in the church of the Spanish mission called the Alamo. They tried to defend themselves against Mexican troops led by Santa Anna. By March 6, Mexican troops had killed all Texans who had fought at the Alamo.

Meanwhile, on March 1, 1836, Texan leaders called a meeting. At the Convention of 1836, lawmakers wrote a Declaration of Independence. The declaration was signed on March 2.

Goliad

Later that month, the Goliad Massacre took place. Mexican soldiers captured James Fannin and many soldiers near Goliad, Texas. Even though the Mexicans promised to show mercy,

Santa Anna ordered the Texans killed. On March 27, about 400 Texan prisoners were shot to death.

Texans were angered by the deaths at the Alamo and at Goliad. They fought even harder for their freedom. Sam Houston, the major general of the Texan army, led a surprise attack on Santa Anna at San Jacinto. Santa Anna surrendered. On May 14, 1836, the Texans and the Mexicans signed the Treaties of Velasco to end the fighting. Finally, Texas was free from Mexican rule.

After the battle at the Alamo, Texans fought even harder for their freedom. Texans have preserved the Alamo as a reminder of the heroes who died for Texas' freedom.

Sam Houston

Texans remember Sam Houston for his bravery at the Battle of San Jacinto in April 1836. Houston, with a wounded ankle, met with Mexican General Antonio López de Santa Anna, who surrendered and ordered Mexican troops to leave Texas. Later, Houston became known by the nickname "Old Sam Jacinto."

At more than 6 feet (1.8 meters) tall, Houston's height helped him become a forceful figure in early Texas politics. After leading Texas' fight for freedom, Houston became president of the Republic of Texas. In 1859, Houston became governor of the state of Texas.

Republic of Texas

Texas was its own country from 1836 to 1845. Sam Houston was the first elected president of the Republic of Texas.

During this time, Texas offered free land to settlers. People came to raise cotton and cattle.

Many Texans wanted Texas to become a state, but Texas allowed slavery. The U.S. Congress argued about admitting another slave state to the Union. Congress also feared that Mexico could become angry with the United States if Texas became a state. These fears kept Texas from being a state until 1845.

On December 29, 1845, Texas finally became the 28th state. Texans chose J. Pinckney Henderson as governor. The southern border of Texas was set at the Rio Grande.

Fighting Wars

The Mexican government was not happy that Texas was a state. It said the Treaties of Velasco were not lawful and that Texas was still a part of Mexico. It also wanted the Texas border farther north at the Nueces River.

Mexico and the United States began the Mexican War (1846–1848). The U.S. Army captured Mexico City in 1847. The Treaty of Guadalupe Hidalgo was signed in 1848 to end the war. Texas remained a state in the United States.

The problems with Mexico were over, but new problems in the United States were beginning. The questions of states' rights and slavery divided the country. When the Civil War (1861–1865) began, Texas left the Union and joined the Confederate States of America.

In 1863, the Confederate army forced the Union army out of Galveston. The Battle of Palmito Ranch, the last battle of the Civil War, was fought in Texas on May 12 and 13, 1865. Even though the war had ended a month earlier, the news had not yet reached Texas.

The period of Reconstruction (1865–1877) after the Civil War was difficult. Even after the state was readmitted to the Union in 1870, some Texans protested giving rights to former slaves. Whites attacked African Americans. During this time, groups of African American soldiers called buffalo soldiers became important members of the U.S. Army.

Cowboys and Cattle Drives

Texas began supplying beef to the rest of the country. Early settlers had brought cattle to Texas. When U.S. settlers came to Texas, the Mexicans taught them riding, roping, herding, and branding. After the Civil War, Texans took advantage of their cattle skills. Cattle sold for up to $40 in the eastern United States. Cowboys herded more than 6 million cattle to the Midwest between 1867 and 1887.

Cattle drives became less common after a railroad was built through Texas in the 1880s. Between 1879 and 1889, Texas added more than 6,000 miles (9,656 kilometers) of railroad tracks across the state. Texans began shipping cattle by train.

Cowboys herded a large number of cattle from Texas into the Midwest during the late 1800s.

Texas Rangers

In 1823, Stephen Austin formed the Texas Rangers to protect settlers from American Indians and bandits. The rangers supplied their own horses and equipment. In 1835, they earned $1.25 per day. Whites, Hispanics, and American Indians all became members of the Texas Rangers.

During the Mexican War (1846–1848), many Mexicans called the Rangers "the Texas Devils." For many years after the war, the Rangers helped keep peace in Texas by fighting bank robbers, cattle thieves, and murderers. Today, more than 100 Rangers investigate serious crimes.

Oil

At the start of the 1900s, a huge discovery changed Texas. Pattillo Higgins and his business partners were certain there was oil beneath the ground on Spindletop Hill near Beaumont. After several failed drilling attempts, they finally struck oil in 1901. The discovery was the beginning of the oil industry in Texas. By 1928, Texas was the top oil producing state in the country. In 1930, C. M. Joiner opened the East Texas oil field, the largest oil field in the world at that time. Many people who found oil became wealthy.

The Spindletop gusher was the first large discovery of oil in Texas. After the discovery, many Texans became wealthy by drilling for oil.

Texans who did not strike oil struggled during the Great Depression (1929–1939). The Texas economy grew stronger during World War II (1939–1945). Its oil, grain, cotton, and beef were in demand.

Modern Texas

The airplane industry helped Texas lead the nation's aerospace industry in the 1960s. In 1962, the National Aeronautics and Space Administration (NASA) developed the Lyndon B. Johnson Space Center near Houston. Mission Control

scientists and engineers supported Apollo astronauts who went to the Moon.

In the 1980s, oil prices fell, and the state's economy weakened. After oil became less valuable, the state changed its economy. Jobs in health care and technology became more important.

In July 2002, heavy rains fell across Texas. Rivers flooded in the Edwards Plateau, as well as San Antonio and New Braunfels. Several people died. Damages to houses and property were about $1 billion.

Houston, Texas, is the site of the Lyndon B. Johnson Space Center. Scientists and engineers at Mission Control, shown here, work to support astronauts on space missions.

The Texas capitol is the tallest capitol building in the United States. It is even taller than the U.S. Capitol in Washington, D.C.

Chapter 4

Government and Politics

The Texas capitol is the largest state capitol building in the United States. The building has 392 rooms, 924 windows, and 404 doors. Completed in 1888, it took about six years to build. Texas red granite covers the outside of the capitol. The inside walls are made of Texas limestone. Copper covers the 85,000-square foot (7,900-square meter) roof.

Texas adopted its first state constitution in 1845. The government wrote new constitutions in 1861, 1866, 1869, and 1876. Amendments can change the Texas constitution. Two-thirds of the state's lawmakers must vote to pass amendments. Next, half of the state's voters must vote for the amendment before the constitution can be changed.

"The power I exert on the court depends on the power of my arguments, not on my gender."

—Sandra Day O'Connor, the first woman named to the U.S. Supreme Court, born in El Paso, Texas

Members of the legislature make laws. The Texas senate has 31 members who serve four-year terms. The Texas house of representatives has 150 members who serve two-year terms. The legislature meets during odd-numbered years.

The governor is the leader of the executive branch. He or she serves four-year terms. The governor signs bills into law or refuses them with a veto. He or she also prepares the state budget and suggests laws.

The Texas judicial branch includes many courts. The chief justice and eight associate justices on the Texas Supreme Court serve six-year terms. The supreme court rules on cases involving civil rights. The top court for criminal cases is the Court of Criminal Appeals. District courts hear local cases.

Key Issues

A great deal of the money needed to run the Texas government comes from taxes. A sales tax raises most tax

Texas' State Government

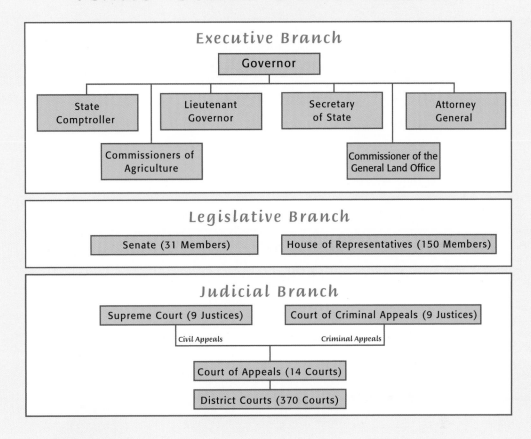

Executive Branch

Governor

State Comptroller · Lieutenant Governor · Secretary of State · Attorney General

Commissioners of Agriculture · Commissioner of the General Land Office

Legislative Branch

Senate (31 Members) · House of Representatives (150 Members)

Judicial Branch

Supreme Court (9 Justices) · Court of Criminal Appeals (9 Justices)

Civil Appeals · Criminal Appeals

Court of Appeals (14 Courts)

District Courts (370 Courts)

money. Texas also charges a tax on fuel. Companies that produce petroleum, natural gas, and other products pay a tax. Texas is one of the 10 states that does not charge an income tax.

Texas takes a tough stand on crime. Criminals who use a gun to commit a crime face longer sentences than those who do not use guns. People guilty of serious crimes face the death penalty. Texas has led the country in the number of executions since 1976. In July 2002, more than 450 people were on death row in Texas.

The Texas Education Agency controls education in Texas. The agency works on ways to improve education. It keeps track of student scores on the Texas Assessment of Knowledge

Texas is working to improve its education system. Many students in south Texas speak Spanish at home. Educators must decide whether these students should be taught in Spanish or English at school.

Six Flags over Texas

Texas' government has changed often during its history. The area has been controlled by six countries. At different times in history, the flags of Spain, France, Mexico, the Republic of Texas, the Confederate States of America, and the United States of America have flown over Texas.

and Skills test. Test scores in 2001 were higher than in earlier years. Fewer students dropped out of school.

Texas changed its welfare system in 1995. It limited the length of time people could be on welfare. The state helps people find jobs and learn skills. One of the poorest areas in the United States is the Rio Grande area. About half the people in this area are poor. Federal and local programs help these people learn job skills to earn money.

Texan Politicians

Several U.S. presidents lived in Texas before going to the White House. Dwight Eisenhower from Denison, Texas, served as president from 1953 to 1961. Lyndon Johnson,

Dwight Eisenhower from Denison, Texas, served in World War II before serving as U.S. president from 1953 to 1961.

the 36th president, served in the U.S. House of Representatives and U.S. Senate before becoming vice president. He became president in 1963 after President John F. Kennedy was shot and killed in Dallas. Originally from Massachusetts, George Bush moved to Texas before becoming Ronald Reagan's vice president, serving from 1981 to 1989. He served as president from 1989 to 1993. His son, George W. Bush, was governor of Texas until he began serving as president in 2001.

Texan women also are involved in politics. In 1924, voters elected Miriam Ferguson to be the first female governor of Texas. She was the second female governor in the United

States. In 1966, Barbara Jordan became the first African American woman elected to the Texas senate. In 1993, Kay Bailey Hutchison became the first female U.S. senator from Texas.

Barbara Jordan served in the Texas senate for six years. In 1972, she became the first African American woman from the South to be elected to the U.S. House of Representatives.

The economy of Texas has relied on oil and agriculture for many years.

Chapter 5

Economy and Resources

In the past, the economy of Texas relied on oil and agriculture. Recently, service industries and manufacturing have played larger parts in the state's economy.

Oil

Oil became a major industry after the discovery on Spindletop Hill. Two-thirds of the land in Texas covers oil fields. One-third of the petroleum in the country lies under Texas soil. Most of the state's petroleum is in the west-central part of Texas.

Oil is not the only natural resource in Texas. The state is the country's top natural gas producer. Limestone and iron ore are also found across the state. Texas has more mining jobs than any other state.

Agriculture

Farming and ranching were the top industries in Texas before 1900. Farmers had a great deal of land. The land between the Rio Grande and San Antonio was especially good for farming.

Today, about three-fourths of the state is farmland. Texas has the most cattle of any state. Two-thirds of the state's farmland is used for cattle ranches. Brangus, Hereford, and Brahman crossbreeds are three main types of cattle.

The rest of Texas' farmland is used for growing crops. The state's main crop is cotton. Texas is the country's top cotton-producing state. It also is the country's top state in hay production. Texas is one of the few states to grow large amounts of rice.

Barbed Wire

In the 1870s, barbed wire changed Texas forever. It closed off the open range, ending cattle drives.

Texas farmers had tried digging ditches and building mud fences to keep cattle away from crops. They even planted thorny bushes to keep cattle from roaming freely across pastures. Nothing was strong enough.

In 1874, Joseph F. Glidden of Illinois twisted steel wire together, making sharp thornlike barbs. When Texas farmers saw that barbed wire could hold back a herd of longhorn cattle, they bought large amounts of the wire to protect their land.

Service Industries

Finance, trade, and community services employ the most workers in Texas. Much of the state's economic growth is due to service industries.

Companies in Texas sell products to other areas of the country. Retail stores that sell clothing or electronics are based in Texas. Insurance companies also have headquarters in Texas.

Manufacturing

Manufacturing plants in Texas prepare soft drinks, baked goods, and computers. Dr Pepper/Seven Up, Inc., the company that makes Dr Pepper and 7 UP soft drinks is based in Plano, Texas. It has many bottling plants, including one in Dublin, Texas, which has been bottling Dr Pepper since 1891.

Texas factories make chemicals for paint, ink, makeup, and fertilizer. Plants in Houston, Corpus Christi, and Beaumont are major producers of chemicals.

Many states have lost manufacturing jobs since 1990, but Texas has not. Texas added more than 25,000 manufacturing jobs between 1990 and 2001. Dallas, Houston, and San Antonio are other important manufacturing cities.

Workers in Texas factories make chemicals that are used in paint, ink, makeup, and fertilizer.

Texans enjoy cooking
meat and vegetables
on outdoor grills.

Chapter 6

People and Culture

When Russian President Vladimir Putin visited the United States in 2001, he rode in President George W. Bush's pickup truck on his Texas ranch. Putin ate southern-fried catfish and put Texas onion butter on his corn bread muffins. For dessert, he ate pecan pie. Bush wanted to give Putin a taste of Texas.

Texas is famous for its chili and its barbecue. San Marcos, Terlingua, Luckenbach, and other cities host chili-cooking contests. Barbecued beef and pork ribs are other tasty Texas dishes.

The food in Texas also reflects the state's Spanish heritage. Enchiladas, fajitas, tamales, and tortillas are Mexican dishes.

European Backgrounds and Hispanic Customs

About 52 percent of the people in Texas are white. People from Germany and France came to live in Texas in the 1800s. In the late 1800s, many people came into Texas through Galveston. It was the country's second largest port for immigrants. The Cajun and Creole people in eastern Texas have French ancestors.

Spanish people brought their language and customs to the area. About 32 percent of the people in Texas are of Hispanic heritage. Many people who live near the Texas and Mexico border speak both Spanish and English.

Other Heritages

African Americans, American Indians, and Asians are minorities in Texas. African Americans make up about 12 percent of the Texas population. Many of their families came to Texas as slaves. The state has three American Indian reservations. The Tigua and Texas Kickapoo live along the Rio Grande. The Alabama-Coushatta live in eastern Texas. Only 3 percent of Texans are Asian. Men came from China to help build railroads. They stayed in Texas with their families after the railroads were finished. Many settled in Houston.

Texas' Ethnic Background

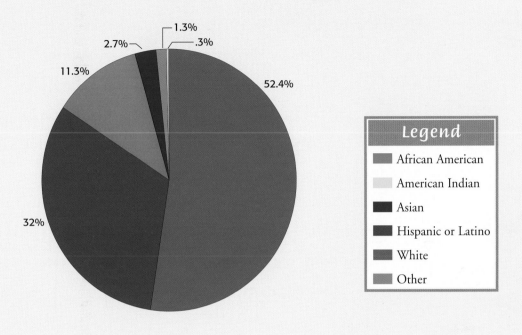

Legend
- African American
- American Indian
- Asian
- Hispanic or Latino
- White
- Other

1.3%
.3%
2.7%
11.3%
52.4%
32%

Immigrants still arrive in Texas from all over the world. Ten percent of the people in Texas were not born in the United States.

Texas is growing rapidly. Its population has doubled since 1960. Beginning in the 1950s, the population of Texas shifted away from rural areas. Today, more than 80 percent of the people in Texas live in city areas. Most of these people live in the eastern half of the state in cities such as Dallas, Fort Worth, San Antonio, and Houston. Houston is the largest city in Texas.

Festivals and Celebrations

Festivals in Texas celebrate the state's history. Every summer, "TEXAS," a musical drama in Palo Duro Canyon State Park, showcases the state's history. In Gonzales, Texas' first battle for freedom from Mexico is remembered during October's Come and Take It festival.

Juneteenth celebrates June 19, 1865, the day many Texan slaves learned they had been freed. In 1979, it became a state holiday. Today, the holiday includes picnics, parades, barbecues, and baseball games.

Big Tex, a 52-foot (16-meter) cowboy statue, welcomes about 3 million visitors to the State Fair of Texas every October. The fair is the largest yearly fair in the United States. People come to hear country music and enjoy the 212-foot (65-meter) Ferris wheel.

Sports

Besides rodeo, Texans enjoy a wide variety of sports. Texas has two pro baseball teams. The Houston Astros play in the National League. From 1965 until 2000, they played in the

The Texas Rangers baseball team plays in the Ballpark in Arlington. This stadium features a baseball museum, a children's learning center, and an office building.

Houston Astrodome. Today, they play at Minute Maid Stadium. The Texas Rangers play in the American League. Their home stadium is in Arlington.

Football is one of the biggest sports in Texas. Texas has two pro football teams, the Houston Texans and the Dallas Cowboys. The Cowboys have won the Super Bowl five times. In 2002, the Texans took the place of the Houston Oilers, who moved to Nashville, Tennessee, in 1997.

Three pro basketball teams play in Texas. The Houston Rockets won the NBA championship in 1994 and 1995. The

Even though the days of cattle drives have ended, modern cowboys include men and women who combine old techniques with modern technology.

San Antonio Spurs won the NBA title in 1999. The Dallas Mavericks have made it to the finals once, losing to the Los Angeles Lakers in 1988.

Cowboys in Texas

Since the days of cattle drives, the idea of the cowboy has interested people around the world. The cowboy is known for his strength and determination. In truth, the first Texas cowboys were men and women. They were European, African American, and Mexican. Their sense of adventure brought them to the wide, open land of Texas.

Cattle drives have ended, but modern cattle ranchers carry on the cowboy way of life. Modern cattle ranchers must know more than how to herd cattle. They also need to know how to run a business. They use helicopters to round up cattle, electric irons to brand cattle, and computers to keep records.

Cowboys, oil, and astronauts are all part of the Texas landscape. The state has rich farmland and empty deserts. It also has rocky mountains, deep river valleys, and wet swamps. Texans are proud of their large, diverse state.

Recipe: Texas Pecan Pie

The pecan tree is the state tree of Texas. These trees grow across most of the state. Some farmers in Texas grow pecans to sell. You can make a delicious pie using pecans.

Ingredients

3 eggs, lightly beaten
½ cup (120 mL) sugar
1 cup (240 mL) light corn
    syrup
1 cup (240 mL) pecan halves
⅛ teaspoon (.6 mL) salt
1 teaspoon (5 mL) vanilla
unbaked pie shell in a pan

Equipment

medium bowl
dry-ingredient measuring
    cups
liquid measuring cup
mixing spoon
measuring spoons
oven mitts

What You Do

1. Heat oven to 425°F (220°C).

2. Mix eggs, sugar, and corn syrup in a medium bowl. Blend well with mixing spoon.

3. With a mixing spoon, stir in pecans, salt, and vanilla.

4. Pour the mixture into the unbaked pie shell.

5. Put the filled pie shell into the oven. Bake at 425°F (220°C) for 10 minutes. Lower the heat to 350°F (180°C) and continue baking for 30 more minutes.

6. Use oven mitts to remove pie from oven. Allow pie to cool before serving.

Makes 6 to 8 servings

Texas' Flag and Seal

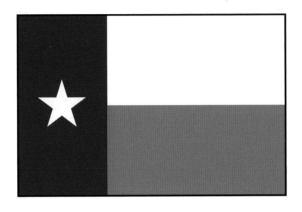

Texas' Flag

The Lone Star Flag was adopted in 1839. It has a white stripe above a red stripe. The white stripe stands for purity, and the red stripe stands for bravery. A blue stripe on the side of the flag means loyalty. A star is in the center of the blue stripe. It stands for Texas' independence.

Texas' State Seal

Texas adopted a state seal in 1839. One star is in the center. This star stands for the time when Texas was its own country. An oak branch and acorns are on one side of the star. This part stands for strength. An olive branch, standing for peace, is on the other side.

Almanac

Nickname: Lone Star State

Population: 20,851,820 (U.S. Census 2000)
Population rank: 2nd

Capital: Austin

Largest cities: Houston, Dallas, San Antonio, Austin, El Paso

Agricultural products: Cotton, wheat, vegetables, citrus fruits, pecans, peanuts, milk, greenhouse plants, eggs, cattle, sheep, hogs, chickens

Average summer temperature: 81 degrees Fahrenheit (27 degrees Celsius)

Average winter temperature: 48 degrees Fahrenheit (9 degrees Celsius)

Average annual precipitation: 30 inches (76 centimeters)

Area: 268,581 square miles (695,625 square kilometers)
Size rank: 2nd

Highest point: Guadalupe Peak, 8,749 feet (2,667 meters) above sea level

Lowest point: Gulf of Mexico, sea level

Pecan tree

Mockingbird

Bird: Mockingbird

Flower: Bluebonnet

Large mammal: Longhorn

Motto: Friendship

Plant: Prickly pear cactus

Natural resources: Oil, natural gas, crushed stone, lime, salt

Types of industry: Industrial machinery and equipment, foods, electrical and electronic products, chemicals, clothing

Small mammal: Armadillo

Song: "Texas, Our Texas" by Gladys Y. Wright and William J. Marsh

Sport: Rodeo

Tree: Pecan

First governor: J. Pinckney Henderson

Statehood: December 29, 1845 (28th state)

U.S. Representatives: 32

U.S. Senators: 2

U.S. electoral votes: 34

Counties: 254

Timeline

State History

1519
Caddo, Apache, and Comanche Indians are living in area; Alonso Alvarez de Pineda of Spain sails into the Rio Grande and explores the Texas coast.

1772
San Antonio is named the center of Spanish government in Texas.

1682
Spanish missions are built at Ysleta.

1836
Texas wins freedom from Mexico.

1845
Texas becomes the 28th state on December 29.

U.S. History

1775–1783
American colonists and the British fight the Revolutionary War.

1620
Pilgrims establish a colony in the New World.

1846–1848
The United States and Mexico fight the Mexican War.

1861–1865
The Union and the Confederacy fight the Civil War.

58

1901

The discovery of oil on Spindletop Hill begins the Texas oil age.

2001

Former Texas governor George W. Bush is sworn in as the 43rd president.

1963

Texan Lyndon B. Johnson becomes the 36th president after President John F. Kennedy is killed in Dallas.

1929–1939

The United States experiences the Great Depression.

1964

U.S. Congress passes the Civil Rights Act, which makes discrimination illegal.

1914–1918

World War I is fought; the United States enters the war in 1917.

1939–1945

World War II is fought; the United States enters the war in 1941.

2001

On September 11, terrorists attack the World Trade Center and the Pentagon.

Words to Know

aerospace (AIR-oh-spayss)—having to do with the science and technology of jet flight or space travel

agriculture (AG-ruh-kul-chur)—farming and ranching

barb (BARB)—a sharp, thornlike point

endangered (en-DAYN-jurd)—at risk of dying out

Hispanic (hiss-PAN-ik)—coming from a country where Spanish is spoken; people of Hispanic origin are called Hispanics.

industry (IN-duh-stree)—a type of business or trade

irrigation (ihr-uh-GAY-shuhn)—supplying water to crops using channels or pipes or other methods

jaguarundi (jahg-wah-RUHN-dee)—a slender, long-tailed wildcat

mesquite (me-SKEET)—a small tree or spiny plant that grows in the Southwest; its wood is used to grill food to give it extra flavor.

petroleum (puh-TROH-lee-uhm)—a thick, oily liquid found below Earth's surface; petroleum is made into gasoline.

To Learn More

Boraas, Tracey. *Sam Houston: Soldier and Statesman.* Let Freedom Ring. Mankato, Minn.: Bridgestone Books, 2003.

Heinrichs, Ann. *Texas.* America the Beautiful. New York: Children's Press, 1999.

Heinrichs, Ann. *Texas.* This Land Is Your Land. Minneapolis: Compass Point Books, 2002.

Isaacs, Sally Senzell. *Life at the Alamo.* Picture the Past. Chicago: Heinemann Library, 2002.

Internet Sites

Track down many sites about Texas.
Visit the FACT HOUND at *http://www.facthound.com*

IT IS EASY! IT IS FUN!
1) Go to *http://www.facthound.com*
2) Type in: 0736815945
3) Click on "FETCH IT" and FACT HOUND will find several links hand-picked by our editors.

Relax and let our pal FACT HOUND do the research for you!

Places to Write and Visit

Brazoria National Wildlife Refuge
1212 North Velasco
P.O. Drawer 1088
Angleton, TX 77516

Dr Pepper Museum
300 South Fifth Street
Waco, TX 76701

Office of the Governor
State Insurance Building
1100 San Jacinto
P.O. Box 12428
Austin, TX 78711-2428

San Jacinto Battleground State Historic Site
3523 Battleground Road
LaPorte, TX 77571

Texas Historical Commission
1511 Colorado
P.O. Box 12276
Austin, TX 78711-2276

Bluebonnets, the state flowers of Texas, bloom in spring, covering many Texas fields with bright blue blossoms.

Index